NATURE'S CHILDREN

LIONS

by Jennifer Zeiger

Children's Press®

An Imprint of Scholastic Inc.
New York   Toronto   London   Auckland   Sydney
Mexico City   New Delhi   Hong Kong
Danbury, Connecticut

Content Consultant
Dr. Stephen S. Ditchkoff
Professor of Wildlife Sciences
Auburn University
Auburn, Alabama

Photographs © 2012: age fotostock/S Meyers: 24; Bob Italiano:
44 foreground, 45 foreground; Dreamstime: 4, 5 background,
20 (Jean-marc Strydom), cover (Paul Maguire), 2, 3 background,
44 background, 45 background (Piccaya); Media Bakery: 15 (Roine
Magnusson), 40; National Geographic Image Collection/Mattias Klum:
32, 39; Photolibrary/C & M Denis-Huot/Peter Arnold Images: 12;
Shutterstock, Inc.: 19 (EcoPrint), 31 (Eric Gevaert), 1, 7 (JI de Wet),
11 (Linn Currie), 5 top, 8 (Mogens Trolle), 23 (Noam Wind),
27 (Steffen Foerster Photography); Superstock: 28 (age fotostock),
36 (imagebroker.net), 3 inset, 5 bottom, 16, 35 (Minden Pictures).

Library of Congress Cataloging-in-Publication Data
Zeiger, Jennifer.
  Lions/by Jennifer Zeiger.
      p. cm.—(Nature's children)
  Includes bibliographical references and index.
  ISBN-13: 978-0-531-20903-5 (lib. bdg.)
    ISBN-10: 0-531-20903-2 (lib. bdg.)
  ISBN-13: 978-0-531-21078-9 (pbk.)
    ISBN-10: 0-531-21078-2 (pbk.)
  1. Lion—Juvenile literature. I. Title. II. Series.
  QL737.C23Z45 2012
  599.757—dc23   2011031077

All rights reserved. Published in 2012 by Children's Press, an imprint
of Scholastic Inc.
Printed in China 62
SCHOLASTIC, CHILDREN'S PRESS, and associated logos are
trademarks and/or registered trademarks of Scholastic Inc.

1 2 3 4 5 6 7 8 9 10 R 21 20 19 18 17 16 15 14 13 12

Lions

Class	Mammalia
Order	Carnivora
Family	Felidae
Genus	*Panthera*
Species	*Panthera leo*
World distribution	Parts of Africa and western India
Habitats	Dry, hot grasslands; forests
Distinctive physical characteristics	Short fur is usually yellow-gold; long tail; most males have long, shaggy manes around their necks
Habits	Live together in groups called prides; work together to protect territory and take down prey; females do most of the hunting
Diet	Antelope, zebra, wildebeest, and other hoofed animals; also known to eat rodents on occasion

Contents

CHAPTER 1

What Is a Lion?

Around the world, the lion is known as King of the Beasts. This powerful, majestic animal has been a symbol of strength and bravery for thousands of years. What makes lions such special animals?

Lions are enormous. They are the largest cats in Africa and the second largest in the world. Only tigers are bigger. Female lions can weigh as much as 400 pounds (181 kilograms). Males are even larger. They can weigh as much as 500 pounds (227 kg). Male lions' distinctive **manes** make them look even bigger. This size comes in handy. A lion is powerful enough to bring down an animal twice its size.

Adult male
6 ft. (1.8 m)

Lion
4 ft. (1.2 m)

Manes make it easy to tell male lions from females.

Loud and Proud

Lions are the loudest cats in the world. A lion's roar can be heard as far as 5 miles (8 kilometers) away. A lion roars to declare ownership of its territory or show its strength. A roar can warn other animals to stay away. Sometimes lions roar together to show how big their group is. This can scare other lions away. A lion might also roar as a way to call other nearby lions.

Lions are very social animals. This is rare among cats. Most cats prefer to live alone. Lions are the only species of cat to live in groups. These groups are called prides. Even when male lions grow up and leave their prides, they are not alone. They bring a few brothers along with them. These groups of wandering male lions then search for other prides to claim as their own.

FUN FACT! Lions sleep up to 24 hours at a time.

A roaring lion is a fearsome sight.

CHAPTER 2

Savanna Survival

Most lions live in the hot, dry African savanna. Lions have to be careful not to overheat. They do not sweat to keep cool as humans do. They find other ways to cool off.

Lions spend a lot of time resting. Running, jumping, and other physical activities cause a lion's body to heat up. The lion can keep its body heat lower by lying still. The best place for lions to rest is in the shade, out of direct sunlight. Lions might rest under a tree or even up in its branches. They might lie in each other's shadows. Lying on their sides also helps cool them off. Heat is lost more quickly through the thin skin of their bellies.

Lions also stay cool by hunting at night. Temperatures are much lower when the sun is down.

Lions often rest with other lions after eating.

Excellent Hunters

Lions are predators. They hunt and eat other animals. Lions rely mainly on their excellent eyesight when they are hunting. Their eyes are sharp, which helps them hunt at night. They also have strong senses of smell and hearing. These senses help them find and bring down their prey.

Lions' powerful legs allow them to run as fast as 36 miles (58 km) per hour. This helps them chase their prey over short distances. A lion's large paws and sharp claws allow it to grab hold of the animal and bring it down.

Lions can also grab on to animals using their long, sharp teeth. Once the prey has been brought down, the lions can eat. They use their claws to keep hold of the prey as they eat. This prevents other lions from stealing the food.

Lions often hunt very large animals.

Competition

Lions have no natural predators in the wild. Most of the threats to them come from other lions.

Normally, one to three male lions claim control of a pride. They help protect the pride from intruders. They mark their territory by spraying urine mixed with their personal scent. These scents tell lions from outside the pride and other animals that the territory is claimed. If another lion crosses the boundary and comes too close to the pride, the lions in the pride will fight it. Males only fight against other males. Females only fight against other females.

Sometimes, a younger male from outside the pride might try to take over. It challenges the pride's dominant male to a fight. The lions use their sharp teeth and claws to bite and swipe at each other. The fight does not always end with one of the lions dying. But the loser can come away with serious injuries. These injuries may not heal and can cause the lion to die later on.

Lions are very aggressive when they fight each other over territory.

Protecting the Cubs

If the male from outside the pride wins the fight, the other males are forced out. The new dominant male then kills the pride's cubs. These cubs belonged to other males. If they are killed, **offspring** of the new dominant male can be born. This gives the male more control over the pride.

The cubs' mothers defend them, but lionesses generally give in to the dominant males in the end. The males are larger and stronger than the females. They will be good protectors of the pride.

Lionesses don't give up so easily if other animals threaten their cubs. Lionesses with cubs stick together in a group called a **crèche**. This group works together to protect the cubs. Sometimes hyenas or other animals will try to hunt and kill cubs. The crèche fights them off. If there are too many intruders, the pride's adult males join in the fight.

Lions often kill hyenas but almost never eat them.

CHAPTER 3

Life in the Pride

Most lions live in Africa. African lions live south of the Sahara, a desert that stretches across northern Africa. The largest populations are in eastern, central, and southern Africa. Lions also live in West Africa. A small population lives in India. These lions live in a protected area of western India's Gir Forest.

Some lions live in dry woodland areas. But most live in grasslands. These areas are often very dry. The grass is tall, and there are few trees.

A pride's territory is important. Territories must include enough water for the pride. They must also include plenty of prey animals for the lions to hunt. If lots of water and prey are available, a territory can be small. Some are as small as 8 square miles (20 sq km). A territory must be bigger if there is not as much food or water. The largest territories can cover up to 155 square miles (400 sq km).

Lions living in dry areas get most of their water from small puddles and ponds.

Working Together

A pride usually includes between four and twelve lionesses. Most of these females are related and include several generations. One to three males are also part of the pride. They patrol the territory and mate with the lionesses to produce cubs. The pride is sometimes scattered in small groups across the territory. These groups come together to hunt. The groups share a large meal when a hunt is particularly successful.

Lionesses do most of the hunting. They are especially good at hunting animals that travel in herds. These include antelopes, wildebeests, and zebras. They also hunt larger prey such as elephants or water buffalos. Sometimes they even steal food from hyenas or other animals.

When hunting, lions stalk an animal and wait for the right moment to strike. Then they chase it to separate it from its herd. Finally, they surround it and bring it down.

Lionesses' coloring allows them to blend in with the environment and stay hidden as they hunt.

Sharing Dinner

The male lions of the pride usually eat first. They force their way toward a kill and push other lions out of the way. A male lion needs to eat about 15 pounds (7 kg) of food each day. But it can eat as much as 75 pounds (34 kg) at once. There is a good reason for this. Lions are not always successful when they hunt. They do not hunt every day. Lions sometimes go more than a day without eating at all. A large amount eaten in one sitting can last them several days.

The pride's lionesses eat after the males have had their fill. Stronger females take the best feeding spots. Weaker ones are forced to take whatever is left over. Finally, the cubs eat after all of the adult lions have finished. Cubs eat whatever scraps are left behind.

FUN FACT! Lions are very good swimmers.

Lions watch to make sure other lions don't try to steal food from them.

Bringing Up Baby

A lioness is pregnant for about 15 weeks before giving birth. She looks for a **secluded** area during this time. Here she will give birth to her **litter** and keep the cubs safe for the first weeks of their lives.

A litter usually has between two and four cubs. The cubs are born blind and defenseless. Their fur is covered in dark brown or black spots. These spots disappear within about 10 months. Because the cubs cannot protect themselves, their mother rarely leaves them alone. She only leaves to find food and water for herself. Hyenas and other predators might find and kill the cubs. Less than half of all cubs survive to become adults.

After about eight weeks, the cubs are strong enough to join the rest of the pride. Many lionesses give birth around the same time. These lionesses form the crèche. They raise their cubs together. Cubs often drink milk from any of the mothers in the crèche.

A single crèche can contain many cubs.

Growing Up

Cubs grow their first adult teeth when they are around 15 weeks old. They can start eating solid food at this point. They start sharing the meat that the older lions eat. Cubs spend a lot of time playing as they grow up. This helps them learn skills they will need when they are adults. They practice by pouncing on bugs, their mothers' tails, and each other. They also play at fighting and wrestling.

Cubs are ready to join in the hunt once they are about 11 months old. They only watch at first. They take more and more active roles over the next few months. Young male lions are usually kicked out of prides when they are around two years old. The brothers wander between territories as they look for new prides to join. Young lionesses usually stay with their mothers' prides. Some split off on their own to start new prides.

Cubs do not actually hurt each other when they wrestle and fight.

28

CHAPTER 4

All in the Family

Lions appear throughout recorded history. Lions took part in the gladiator games of ancient Rome. Ancient Greeks made them a symbol on the star calendar known today as the zodiac.

Two million years ago, lions lived all around the world. They lived in North and South America. They lived all across Africa. They were spread across the Middle East. Lions were even found as far north as the Balkans in Europe.

Things began to change around 10,000 years ago. Lions disappeared from North and South America. Their range in Europe decreased. They disappeared from the Balkans 2,000 years ago. Their range continued to shrink until it became what it is today.

Images of lions can be seen in a wide variety of ancient artworks, including this piece of Roman art.

Cats of All Kinds

Lions are members of the **feline** family. The feline family consists of nearly 40 different species of cats. These include the cheetah, cougar, and lynx. The **domestic** cats that people keep as pets also belong to this family. Cats come in all sizes, from the hand-size rusty spotted cat to the powerful tiger. They can be found in the wild on almost every continent.

Lions are part of the *Panthera* **genus**. Members of this genus are often called big cats. These cats are usually much larger than other felines. They also have the ability to roar. These cats are most common in Africa, Asia, and parts of Central and South America. The lion's closest relatives are the tiger, jaguar, and leopard. In fact, the bodies of lions and tigers are so similar that it is hard to tell the difference between their skeletons.

Like lions, tigers are fierce hunters.

African and Asian Lions

There is only one species of lion. But the species can be separated into two **subspecies**. Most lions belong to the subspecies called African lions. Their cousins in India are called Asian lions. Asian lions are slightly smaller than African lions. Male African lions generally have longer, shaggier manes than male Asian lions do. Asian lion prides also have fewer members. They are often made up entirely of females and cubs.

Smaller differences exist within the African subspecies. Behavior and diet can change depending on a pride's preferences. Some African prides prefer to eat water buffalo or antelope. Others spend their time hunting elephants. Some prides in East Africa have been known to hunt mostly during the day. African lions elsewhere can usually be seen hunting only at night.

Asian lions can be difficult to tell apart from their African relatives.

CHAPTER 5

Lions in Danger

The lion's range and population have become smaller over the past several thousand years. They have decreased at an especially fast rate over the past 150 years. African lions are considered vulnerable. This means the population is smaller than it should be. Scientists believe that there are between 20,000 and 30,000 African lions living in the wild. This is possibly half as many lions as there were 20 years ago. Their range is less than a quarter of what it was 150 years ago.

Asian lions are even more threatened than their African relatives. They are considered endangered. This means they are in danger of becoming extinct if nothing is done to help them. Their populations once stretched throughout India and the Middle East. The lions of India's Gir Forest are the only Asian lions living in the wild today. There are about 200 of them.

The Gir Forest National Park was once hunting grounds for Indian royalty.

Threats

Lions are disappearing for several reasons. Many of these reasons are connected to humans. The world's human population has exploded over the past several centuries. Humans need more space to live and food to eat as their numbers increase. Cities, towns, and farms continue to expand.

Humans sometimes find space by taking over areas where lions live. The prey animals that lions depend on also lose territory. Lions struggle to find food as prey populations decrease. Lions sometimes kill cattle for food. Ranchers and farmers shoot the lions to protect their land and animals. A lion may also be shot if it wanders into a city or town.

Poaching is another major threat to the survival of lions. Poachers hunt lions illegally. They do not follow rules about where to hunt or how many lions can be killed. Other hunters purchase permits and are only allowed to hunt in areas where there are many lions.

African ranchers sometimes kill lions to protect their herds.

Protecting Lions

Many governments and organizations are working to protect lions. One method is to protect the areas where lions live. It is illegal for hunters to enter these protected areas. Farms and ranches cannot expand into protected land. The Gir Forest in India is one example of a protected area. The forest's lions are kept from hunters, farmers, and land developers.

Other organizations look for ways to increase the lion population. This might mean finding a good balance between prey animals and lion populations. This technique would help not only lions, but also the animals they depend on for food.

Increasing the lion population could also mean having to find new places for lions to live. Researchers in India are working on a way to create a second population of Asian lions. These lions would live outside the Gir Forest. This would give Asian lions more space. The population would then stay healthier.

Even the Gir Forest lions have been threatened by poachers.

Looking at Lions

Protected land can also be used to help a country's economy. Many countries open their protected lands to tourists. People from around the world can travel there to see lions living in the wild. These travelers spend money in the cities or villages nearby. A government can use some of this money to continue protecting lions. It can educate its people about the importance of preserving endangered species.

People can also get a closer look at lions by visiting zoos. Lions are often a major attraction at zoos all around the world. Some of these lions have been rescued from dangerous situations in the wild. More often, they are born in zoos. Some zoos work to increase the populations of endangered species in the hope of preventing extinction.

Lions are truly unique creatures. With a little help from humans around the world, this king of beasts will have a bright future.

Safari tours allow people to get a close-up look at lions without bothering them.

Words to Know

crèche (KRESH) — a group of lionesses that all have young cubs around the same age

domestic (duh-MES-tik) — tamed

dominant (DAH-muh-nint) — most influential or powerful

economy (i-KAH-nuh-mee) — the system of buying, selling, making things, and managing money in a place

endangered (en-DAYN-jurd) — at risk of becoming extinct, usually because of human activity

extinct (ik-STINGKT) — no longer found alive

feline (FEE-line) — of or having to do with cats

generations (jen-uh-RAY-shunz) — groups of animals or individuals born around the same time

genus (JEE-nuhs) — a group of related plants or animals that is larger than a species but smaller than a family

grasslands (GRAS-landz) — large, open areas of grass

herds (HURDZ) — groups of animals that stay together or move together

intruders (in-TROO-durz) — people or animals that enter a territory where they are not wanted

litter (LIT-ur) — a number of baby animals that are born at the same time to the same mother

manes (MAYNZ) — the long, thick hair on the heads and necks of lions, horses, and some other animals

mate (MAYT) — to join together to produce babies

offspring (AWF-spring) — the young of an animal or a human being

permits (PUR-mitz) — official documents giving someone permission to do something

poaching (POH-ching) — hunting or fishing illegally

predators (PREH-duh-turz) — animals that live by hunting other animals for food

prey (PRAY) — an animal that's hunted by another animal for food

prides (PRYDZ) — organized groups of lions

range (RAYNJ) — the overall area where an animal can be found

savanna (suh-VAN-uh) — a flat, grassy plain with few or no trees

secluded (si-KLOO-did) — quiet and private, not seen or visited by many people

social (SOH-shul) — preferring to live in groups

species (SPEE-sheez) — one of the groups into which animals and plants of the same genus are divided

stalk (STAWK) — to hunt or track an animal in a quiet, secret way

subspecies (SUB-spee-sheez) — groups of animals that are part of the same species, but share important differences

territory (TER-i-tor-ee) — area of land claimed by an animal

vulnerable (VUHL-nur-uh-buhl) — in a position or condition to be easily damaged

PACIFIC

OCEAN

NORTH

AMERICA

ATLANTIC

SOUTH
AMERICA

Lion Range

ARCTIC OCEAN

EUROPE

ASIA

Asiatic Lion

AFRICA

OCEAN

INDIAN

OCEAN

AUSTRALIA

Find Out More

Books

Joubert, Beverly, and Dereck Joubert. *Face to Face with Lions*. Washington, DC: National Geographic, 2008.

Schafer, Susan. *Lions*. New York: Marshall Cavendish Benchmark, 2010.

Squire, Ann O. *Lions*. New York: Children's Press, 2005.

Web Sites

National Geographic Kids—Lions
http://kids.nationalgeographic.com/kids/animals/creaturefeature/lion/
Learn some amazing facts, watch videos, and even listen to a lion on this site!

Smithsonian National Zoological Park—Great Cats
http://nationalzoo.si.edu/animals/greatcats/lionfacts.cfm
This site includes photos, facts, and even an updated diary about the lions living at the Smithsonian Zoo.

Visit this Scholastic web site for more information on lions:
www.factsfornow.scholastic.com

Index

About the Author

Jennifer Zeiger earned a degree from DePaul University. She now lives in Chicago, Illinois, where she writes and edits books for kids.